A Note From Rick Renner

I am on a personal quest to see a "revival of the Bible" so people can establish their lives on a firm foundation that will stand strong and endure the test as end-time storm winds begin to intensify.

In order to experience a revival of the Bible in your personal life, it is important to take time each day to read, receive, and apply its truths to your life. James tells us that if we will continue in the perfect law of liberty — refusing to be forgetful hearers, but determined to be doers — we will be blessed in our ways. As you watch or listen to the programs in this series and work through this corresponding study guide, I trust you will search the Scriptures and allow the Holy Spirit to help you hear something new from God's Word that applies specifically to your life. I encourage you to be a doer of the Word He reveals to you. Whatever the cost, I assure you — it will be worth it.

> Thy words were found, and I did eat them;
> and thy word was unto me the joy and rejoicing of mine heart:
> for I am called by thy name, O Lord God of hosts.
> — Jeremiah 15:16

Your brother and friend in Jesus Christ,

Rick Renner

A MYSTERY — What the Bible Really Teaches About the Rapture of the Church

Copyright © 2024 by Rick Renner
1814 W. Tacoma St.
Broken Arrow, OK 74012-1406

Published by Rick Renner Ministries
www.renner.org

ISBN 13: 978-1-6675-0997-6

ISBN 13 eBook: 978-1-6675-0998-3

How To Use This Study Guide

This five-lesson study guide corresponds to *"A MYSTERY — What the Bible Really Teaches About the Rapture of the Church" With Rick Renner* (Renner TV). Each lesson in this study guide covers a topic that is addressed during the program series, with questions and references supplied to draw you deeper into your own private study of the Scriptures on this subject.

To derive the most benefit from this study guide, consider the following:

First, watch or listen to the program prior to working through the corresponding lesson in this guide. (Programs can also be viewed at **renner.org** by clicking on the Media/Archives links or on our Renner Ministries YouTube channel.)

Second, take the time to look up the scriptures included in each lesson. Prayerfully consider their application to your own life.

Third, use a journal or notebook to make note of your answers to each lesson's Study Questions and Practical Application challenges.

Fourth, invest specific time in prayer and in the Word of God to consult with the Holy Spirit. Write down the scriptures or insights He reveals to you.

Finally, take action! Whatever the Lord tells you to do according to His Word, do it.

For added insights, it is recommended that you obtain the *Renner Interpretive Version of James and Jude: A Parallel Study Bible for People of Faith* as well as Rick's book *Christmas — The Rest of the Story*. You may also select from Rick's other available resources by placing your order at **renner.org** or by calling 1-800-742-5593.

TOPIC

9 Rapture–Type Events in the Bible

SCRIPTURES

1. **1 Thessalonians 4:15-17** — For this we say unto you by the word of the Lord, that we which are alive and remain unto the coming of the Lord shall not prevent them which are asleep. For the Lord himself shall descend from heaven with a shout, with the voice of the archangel, and with the trump of God: and the dead in Christ shall rise first: then we which are alive and remain shall be caught up together with them in the clouds, to meet the Lord in the air: and so shall we ever be with the Lord.

2. **Genesis 5:24** — And Enoch walked with God: and he was not; for God took him.

3. **Hebrews 11:5** — By faith Enoch was translated that he should not see death; and was not found, because God had translated him: for before his translation he had this testimony, that he pleased God.

4. **2 Kings 2:11** — And it came to pass, as they still went on, and talked, that, behold, there appeared a chariot of fire, and horses of fire, and parted them both asunder; and Elijah went up by a whirlwind into heaven.

5. **Acts 1:9-11** — And when he had spoken these things, while they beheld, he was taken up; and a cloud received him out of their sight. And while they looked stedfastly toward heaven as he went up, behold, two men stood by them in white apparel; which also said, Ye men of Galilee, why stand ye gazing up into heaven? this same Jesus, which is taken up from you into heaven, shall so come in like manner as ye have seen him go into heaven.

6. **Acts 8:39,40** — And when they were come up out of the water, the Spirit of the Lord caught away Philip, that the eunuch saw him no more: and he went on his way rejoicing. But Philip was found at Azotus: and passing through he preached in all the cities, till he came to Caesarea.

7. **2 Corinthians 12:2-4** — I knew a man in Christ above fourteen years ago, (whether in the body, I cannot tell; or whether out of the body, I cannot tell: God knoweth;) such an one caught up to the third heaven. And I knew such a man, (whether in the body, or out of the body, I cannot tell: God knoweth;) how that he was caught up into paradise, and heard unspeakable words, which it is not lawful for a man to utter.

8. **Revelation 4:1,2** — After this I looked, and, behold, a door was opened in heaven: and the first voice which I heard was as it were of a trumpet talking with me; which said, Come up hither, and I will shew thee things which must be hereafter. And immediately I was in the spirit....

9. **1 Thessalonians 4:17** — Then we which are alive and remain shall be caught up together with them in the clouds, to meet the Lord in the air: and so shall we ever be with the Lord.

10. **Revelation 11:11,12** — And after three days and an half the spirit of life from God entered into them, and they stood upon their feet; and great fear fell upon them which saw them. And they heard a great voice from heaven saying unto them, Come up hither. And they ascended up to heaven in a cloud; and their enemies beheld them.

GREEK WORDS

1. "caught up together" — ἁρπάζω (*harpadzo*): to catch, seize, or take away; to snatch suddenly; to snatch just in time

2. "caught away" — ἁρπάζω (*harpadzo*): to catch, seize, or take away; to snatch suddenly; to snatch just in time

SYNOPSIS

The five lessons in this study titled *A MYSTERY — What the Bible Really Teaches About the Rapture of the Church* will focus on the following topics:

- 9 Rapture–Type Events in the Bible
- Mockers in the Last Days
- The Rapture in First Thessalonians
- The Rapture in First Corinthians
- Key Differences Between the Rapture of the Church and the Second Coming of Christ

Today, there are many opinions concerning the topic of the rapture of the Church. Some believe Jesus will return *before* the Tribulation, while others hold to the notion that He will return in the *middle* or at the *end* of the Tribulation. There is even a group of believers who doubt there will even be a rapture.

Regardless of people's opinions, the Rapture is a real, biblical event that is talked about throughout Scripture. From Genesis to Revelation, the Bible offers numerous examples of the rapture, making it an undeniable reality in the life of a believer.

The emphasis of this lesson:

There are nine rapture-type examples found in the Bible. From the Old Testament accounts of Enoch's and Elijah's sudden departures to the ascension of Christ and the catching away of the apostle Paul and the apostle John, the concept of being raptured is repeatedly presented throughout Scripture.

The Doctrine of the 'Rapture' Is Clearly Taught in the Bible

Some have argued that the word "rapture" is not in the Bible, and therefore it is not a real, biblical event. However, when we look at the Vulgate, which is the Latin version of Scripture that was completed by Jerome in about 405 AD and used by believers for hundreds of years, we see that the word "rapture" is a translation of the Latin word *raptura*, and *raptura* is derived from the Greek word *harpadzo*. This word is found in Paul's first letter to the church of Thessalonica, where he describes the rapture of the Church.

Writing under the inspiration of the Holy Spirit, Paul said:

> **For this we say unto you by the word of the Lord, that we which are alive and remain unto the coming of the Lord shall not prevent them which are asleep. For the Lord himself shall descend from heaven with a shout, with the voice of the archangel, and with the trump of God: and the dead in Christ shall rise first: then we which are alive and remain shall be caught up together**

**with them in the clouds, to meet the Lord in the air: and so
shall we ever be with the Lord.**

— 1 Thessalonians 4:15-17

Notice the phrase "caught up together." It is translated from a form of the
Greek word *harpadzo*, and it means *to catch, seize,* or *take away*. It carries
the idea of *snatching suddenly* or *to snatch just in the nick of time*.

When we factor in the original Greek meaning of the key words in First
Thessalonians 4:17, the *Renner Interpretive Version (RIV)* says:

> **Then at that exact synchronized moment, those who are still
> physically alive and who have survived everything — I'm
> talking about the remnant that will still be around and left
> remaining at this time — they will suddenly and supernaturally
> be snatched away out of imminent danger just in the nick
> of time as the Lord instigates a divine rescue operation to
> transport them into the clouds to join those who have been
> resurrected. There in the air's lower atmosphere where the Lord
> has descended to meet them, those who were raised from the
> dead and the remnant who was supernaturally snatched out
> of danger will encounter the Lord. And at that encounter, the
> Lord will roll out the red carpet to give the new arrivals a royal
> reception to match the VIP status He knows they deserve! Then
> and after that, we will always — at all times and forevermore —
> be with the Lord.**

Friend, First Thessalonians 4:17 is a clear description of the Rapture —
the great *catching away* of believers. This "blessed hope" has been cherished
by Christians for thousands of years (*see* Titus 2:13). Specifically, the Early
Church fathers believed and understood the Rapture would be a pre-
Tribulation event and taught along those lines.

For example, **Irenaeus** [c. 130-202 AD], who is recognized as one of the
most substantial early theologians of the Church, said: "When in the end,
the Church shall be suddenly caught up from this, it is said, 'There shall
be tribulation such as has not been since the beginning, neither shall be.'"[1]
It's interesting to note that Irenaeus said the Rapture is going to happen
in the end, and when the Church is suddenly caught up, *then* the Tribulation will begin. This is the doctrine of a pre-Tribulation rapture.

There Are 9 Rapture-Type Events in Scripture

Now there are people who say, "The idea of Christians vanishing into thin air is just a myth or fantasy. It is a pie-in-the-sky belief certain individuals have concocted that is never going to happen. People don't just disappear." Those who argue in this way clearly do not know the Bible. The fact is, from the earliest parts of Genesis to the final book of Revelation, there are several rapture-type examples that the Holy Spirit documented for us to see, and here they are in order of appearance.

1: Enoch

Seven generations after Adam, a man named Enoch was born. The Bible tells us Enoch lived 365 years and had many sons and daughters (*see* Genesis 5:22). But most importantly, Genesis 5:24 says, "And Enoch walked with God: and he was not; for God took him." One day, as Enoch was living in close relationship with God, he was supernaturally snatched out of this world and taken to Heaven, never tasting death.

Hebrews 11:5 says, "By faith Enoch was translated that he should not see death; and was not found, because God had translated him: for before his translation he had this testimony, that he pleased God." Interestingly, the word "found" is translated from a form of the Greek word *heurisko*, which means *to search for*, *to seek for*, and *to thoroughly investigate*, which means people were really looking for Enoch, but they couldn't find him.

Where did he go? The Bible says God translated him — taking him from the realm of the physical to the supernatural dimension of the spirit. Before his translation, he had a reputation of pleasing God. This is the first record of a rapture in Scripture. God raptured Enoch into Heaven.

2: Elijah

The second account of a rapture is found in Second Kings 2:11, where the Bible says, "And it came to pass, as they still went on, and talked, that, behold, there appeared a chariot of fire, and horses of fire, and parted them both asunder; and Elijah went up by a whirlwind into heaven."

The prophet Elijah was physically caught up into Heaven by the Spirit of God. He was translated from the natural realm into the dimension of the spirit via a flaming chariot of fire. Rather than taste death, Elijah was raptured from the earth into the very presence of God.

3: Jesus

The third example of someone being raptured involves Jesus. According to Scripture, He was supernaturally caught up into Heaven 40 days after He had been resurrected from the dead. We read about this amazing event in Acts 1:9-11:

> **And when he had spoken these things, while they beheld, he was taken up; and a cloud received him out of their sight. And while they [the disciples] looked stedfastly toward heaven as he went up, behold, two men stood by them in white apparel; which also said, Ye men of Galilee, why stand ye gazing up into heaven? this same Jesus, which is taken up from you into heaven, shall so come in like manner as ye have seen him go into heaven.**

This passage clearly reveals Jesus Himself was raptured — He was "taken up into the clouds." This is also recorded in Luke 24:51. The Bible says while Jesus was blessing His closest, most devoted followers, He was physically caught up into Heaven, translated from the realm of the natural into the realm of the spirit by the power of God.

4: Philip

When we come to Acts 8, we find another example of someone being raptured. In this case, it was Philip, one of Jesus' apostles. After Philip shared the Good News of Jesus with a high-ranking official of Ethiopia and baptized him in water, the Bible says, "And when they were come up out of the water, the Spirit of the Lord caught away Philip, that the eunuch saw him no more: and he went on his way rejoicing" (Acts 8:39).

The words "caught away" are translated from a form of the Greek word *harpadzo* — the same word used in First Thessalonians 4:17 to describe the rapture of the Church. Philip was supernaturally seized by the Spirit of the Lord and disappeared. The Ethiopian leader saw him no more because Philip was raptured.

Acts 8:40 goes on to tell us "...Philip was found at Azotus: and passing through he preached in all the cities, till he came to Caesarea." Like a scene out of a modern-day sci-fi movie, Philip was supernaturally transported from the road going from Jerusalem to Gaza to the town of Azotus, approximately 20 miles north of where he was. What an extraordinary event to see!

5: Paul

Our next example of a rapture involves the apostle Paul. Speaking to the believers at the church in Corinth, Paul said, "I knew a man in Christ above fourteen years ago, (whether in the body, I cannot tell; or whether out of the body, I cannot tell: God knoweth;) such an one *caught up* to the third heaven. And I knew such a man, (whether in the body, or out of the body, I cannot tell: God knoweth;) how that he was *caught up* into paradise, and heard unspeakable words, which it is not lawful for a man to utter" (2 Corinthians 12:2-4).

Twice in these verses, we see the words "caught up," and in both instances, they are a translation of the Greek word *harpadzo*, which means *to catch*, *seize*, or *take away*. It is the same word used to describe the rapture of the Church in First Thessalonians 4:17 as well as Philip's catching away in Acts 8:39. It indicates that Paul himself experienced a rapture-type event. The Spirit of God snatched him and took him up into the third heaven where he heard indescribable words of truth and revelation from the Lord.

6: John

The sixth rapture in Scripture is described in the book of Revelation. Here we are informed that the apostle John, like Paul, was caught up into Heaven and given a detailed revelation of the seven-year Tribulation, the millennial reign of Christ, and the Great White Throne Judgment.

John began describing his experience by saying, "After this I looked, and, behold, a door was opened in heaven: and the first voice which I heard was as it were of a trumpet talking with me; which said, Come up hither, and I will shew thee things which must be hereafter. And immediately I was in the spirit…" (Revelation 4:1,2).

The voice John heard was that of Jesus, and He told John to "come up hither." Immediately, John was "in the spirit" — he was translated from the realm of the natural into the realm of the supernatural. Like Enoch, Elijah, Jesus, Philip, and Paul, John was snatched up and raptured away.

7: The Church

Up until this point, all the rapture-like events we've examined have already taken place. The next rapture in Scripture that is quickly approaching is the one that involves all believers, and the key verse describing this event is First Thessalonians 4:17, which says:

Then we which are alive and remain shall be caught up together with them in the clouds, to meet the Lord in the air: and so shall we ever be with the Lord.

Just imagine! In the very near future, believers who are faithfully serving God and alive on the earth will one day vanish and be supernaturally *caught up* into the very presence of the Lord Jesus! Again, the words "caught up" are translated from a form of the Greek word *harpadzo*, meaning *to catch, seize,* or *take away*. It carries the idea of *snatching suddenly* or *to snatch just in time.*

8: The Two End-Time Prophets

The eighth rapture recorded in Scripture is the catching away of the two witnesses who will prophesy on God's behalf during the first three and a half years of the Tribulation. When they finish their work of testifying for the Lord, the Bible says the Antichrist will kill them and put their dead bodies on display in the streets of Jerusalem for all the world to see (*see* Revelation 11:7-9).

But these two witnesses won't stay dead! The Bible says, "And after three days and an half the Spirit of life from God entered into them, and they stood upon their feet; and great fear fell upon them which saw them. And they heard a great voice from heaven saying unto them, Come up hither. And they ascended up to heaven in a cloud; and their enemies beheld them" (Revelation 11:11,12).

Just like Jesus, John, Elijah, and the others, these two prophets of God will ascend into Heaven into the very presence of God, giving us yet another example of what being raptured looks like.

9: The Tribulation Saints

During the seven years of Tribulation on earth, there will be people who miraculously come to the saving knowledge of Christ. Interestingly, they too will be raptured into Heaven, and we find this event foretold by the apostle John in Revelation 14:14-16. Jesus Himself will reach into the earth and harvest the souls of those who will be saved during the Tribulation and take them to Heaven with Him. They will be supernaturally, physically caught away into the presence of the Lord.

These nine rapture examples in Scripture all describe a sudden catching away — a snatching or seizing — of individuals or groups that are taken from the earth into Heaven. These accounts are proof that the concept of the Rapture is indeed in the Bible. Six have already taken place, and three are still to come. The very next rapture that is rapidly approaching is the rapture of the Church. At any moment in the very near future, Christ will descend into the lower atmosphere and seize believers into the air with Him, and for eternity we will be with the Lord!

In our next lesson, we will examine what Peter prophesied would happen in the last days just before Christ's return — that mockers will arise and scoff at the idea of the Rapture and claim it to be nonsense.

STUDY QUESTIONS

> Study to shew thyself approved unto God, a workman that
> needeth not to be ashamed, rightly dividing the word of truth.
> — 2 Timothy 2:15

1. According to Titus 2:13, what is the rapture of the church often referred to? How is Titus 2:13 similar to and related to Paul's words of instruction regarding the rapture in First Thessalonians 4:18?
2. Scripture says Elijah was raptured into Heaven in a chariot of fire (*see* 2 Kings 2:11). But according to Second Kings 2:16, what other supernatural occurrences seem to have been a pattern in Elijah's life? As you answer, consider what the apostle Philip experienced while ministering to the Ethiopian official (*see* Acts 8:39,40).

PRACTICAL APPLICATION

> But be ye doers of the word, and not hearers only,
> deceiving your own selves.
> — James 1:22

1. As you begin this study on what the Bible says about the rapture of the Church, what has been your understanding of this subject up until now? What teaching have you heard and held on to?
2. After reading through the nine different rapture events in this lesson, which one stands out to you most? Why is it impactful to you? What are your greatest takeaways overall?

---

[1] Irenaeus, *Against Heresies*, Book V, chap. 29, p. 558, https://ccel.org/ccel/schaff/anf01/ anf01/ Page_558.html.

TOPIC

Mockers in the Last Days

SCRIPTURES

1. **2 Peter 3:3,4** — Knowing this first, that there shall come in the last days scoffers, walking after their own lusts, and saying, Where is the promise of his coming? for since the fathers fell asleep, all things continue as they were from the beginning of creation.

2. **2 Peter 3:8,9** — But, beloved, be not ignorant of this one thing, that one day is with the Lord as a thousand years, and a thousand years as one day. The Lord is not slack concerning his promise, as some men count slackness; but is longsuffering to us-ward, not willing that any should perish, but that all should come to repentance.

GREEK WORDS

1. "knowing this" — γινώσκω (*ginosko*): 'I know,' but the form used here describes what must be known, always known, and never forgotten

2. "first" — πρῶτον (*proton*): first, foremost, or above all else

3. "that" — ὅτι (*hoti*): a conjunction that points expressly to the following important conclusion

4. "the last days" — ἐσχάτων τῶν ἡμερῶν (*eschaton ton hemeron*) — the very end or last of days; here, Peter uses a form of ἔσχατος (*eschatos*), a word that depicts what is final, and where we derive the word "eschatology" — which is the theological study of end times or the study of last things; the word ἔσχατος (*eschatos*) points to the very last or the ultimate end of a thing; used by ancient Greeks to describe the point that was furthest away; the ancient world used the word ἔσχατος (*eschatos*) as a seafaring word to describe the last port of call for a ship; although a ship in transit stops at many ports en route to its final destination, the word ἔσχατος (*eschatos*) was used to depict the very last port, and this last stopping-off point signified that it was the end of the road and the journey was finished; furthermore, ancient writers used ἔσχατος (*eschatos*) to refer to the final boundary of a territory, or the farthest edge of a domain; thus, the word ἔσχατος (*eschatos*)

indicated, This is the end, and you can go no further; in this verse, ἔσχατος (*eschatos*) points to the very ultimate end of days or to the very last of a long last-days season that could be called the last of the last days

5. "scoffers" — ἐμπαιγμονῇ ἐμπαῖκται (*empaigmone empaiktai*): scoffing scoffers; derived from a word that depicts those who make fun of something through mockery; often used for playing a game with children or to amuse a crowd by impersonating someone in a silly and exaggerated way; used to depict a game of charades when someone intends to comically portray or even make fun of someone; Peter uses this word to foretell a day at the very end of the age when scoffers would rise up before Jesus returns to mock people who still believe in Christ's return for the Church

6. "saying" — λέγοντες (*legontes*): pictures one who says, says, and says, or talk that is continuous

7. "where" — ποῦ (*pou*): where, exactly where, in what place, and is used to question whatever is being discussed

8. "the promise" — ἡ ἐπαγγελία (*he epangelia*): the definite article ἡ (*he*) with ἐπαγγελία (*epangelia*), which is the word for an announcement, declaration, or guaranteed promise, and a legal term to describe what has been legally promised and is expected to come to pass; however, Peter uses the definite article ἡ (*he*) to state that the promise of Christ's return is a very specific promise that God has announced, declared, guaranteed, and promised to come to pass; the guaranteed promise of Christ's return was an integral part of apostolic preaching and teaching

9. "coming" — παρουσία (*parousia*): a technical expression for the royal visit of a king or emperor who has come with all the power, might, and authority to deal with a situation and put everything in order; used interchangeably to describe both the Rapture of the Church and the Second Coming of Christ; to know how παρουσία (*parousia*) is being used depends on the context of surrounding verses, but here Peter uses this word to refer to the long-promised rapture of the Church

10. "the fathers" — οἱ πατέρες (*hoi pateres*): this could refer to the earliest fathers of the Christian faith, who firmly believed in and declared the promise of Christ's return for the Church at the end of the age; however, it could likewise refer to earlier fathers of the faith — as early as Enoch — who, from the very beginning of time, saw the end of the age and prophesied the eventual return of Christ (*see* Jude 14,15)

11. "continue" — διαμένω (*diameno*): to perpetually and thoroughly remain completely the same and unchanged

12. "as they were" — οὗτως (*houtos*), which means in keeping with; in like manner; in the same manner; exactly the same; and, therefore, consistent and unchanged

13. "beginning" — ἀρχή (*arche*): the beginning of creation or what is the most ancient and archaic of known time

14. "ignorant" — λανθάνω (*lanthano*): to forget, deliberately ignore, purposefully disregard; hence, to completely forget facts that were previously believed or known

15. "slack" — βραδύνω (*braduno*): to be tardy, slow, delayed, or late in time, but specifically refers to lateness in reference to an appointed time; used medically to describe a person who was mentally or physically handicapped, and therefore slow to speak or slow in terms of physical movement; ancient Greek speakers used βραδύνω (*braduno*) to picture a person who is hesitant to act due to either a lack of direction, commitment, or resources; by using this word, the Holy Spirit states that God is not delayed, slow, or tardy regarding the promise that Jesus will return, or furthermore, regarding any promise of a coming judgment

16. "count" — ἡγέομαι (*hegeomai*): conclude, consider, deem, esteem, figure, or suppose

17. "slackness" — βραδύνω (*braduno*): to be tardy, slow, delayed, or late in time, but specifically refers to lateness in reference to an appointed time

18. "longsuffering" — μακροθυμέω (*makrothumeo*): a compound of μακρός (*makros*) and θυμός (*thumos*); the word μακρός (*makros*) depicts what is long or of long duration, similar to a long span of time, while θυμός (*thumos*) means anger and depicts a strong and growing passion; when compounded, it pictures the patient restraint of anger and denotes longsuffering

SYNOPSIS

Have you heard people question or even mock the idea of Jesus returning to rapture His Church? Peter prophesied this would happen in his second letter to believers. The very fact that people are making fun of those who believe in Christ's soon return is a sign we are living in the last of the last days. In this lesson, we will carefully unpack Peter's prophetic warning and examine what its fulfillment means to us today.

The emphasis of this lesson:

Peter's prophecy of scoffers coming in the last days is being fulfilled in our day. Rather than deliberately ignore or willfully forget that Christ's return is imminent, Peter urges us to hold on to the guaranteed promise of His coming, realizing what seems to be a delay is actually an expression of God's patience as He waits for people to repent of their sins.

The Presence of Scoffers Is a Major Sign We Are in the Last Days

When Peter wrote his two letters, he was writing to believers living in the First Century. Under the anointing of the Spirit of God, he pointed all the way to the end of the Church Age — the time in which we are living — and prophesied that scoffers would manifest in the world and even in the Church. He said:

> **Knowing this first, that there shall come in the last days scoffers, walking after their own lusts.**
>
> **— 2 Peter 3:3**

There are several important words to understand in this verse, including the words "knowing this." This phrase is a form of the word *ginosko*, which means *'I know,'* but the form used here describes *what must be known, always known, and never forgotten.* Thus, we could translate Peter's opening words to say, "You need to really know this; you need to always know this; you need to never forget this."

Then Peter adds the word "first" — you must know this *first*. This is the Greek word *proton*, and it means *first, foremost,* or *above all else.* Clearly, what Peter is about to describe is of great importance. He said, "Knowing this first, that…" (2 Peter 3:3). Even the word "that" is significant. It is the little Greek word *hoti*, a conjunction that points expressly to the following conclusion:

> **…There shall come in the last days scoffers, walking after their own lusts.**
>
> **— 2 Peter 3:3**

The 'Last Days' Describes
the Ultimate End of the Age

The words "the last days" are a translation of the Greek phrase *eschaton ton hemeron*, which could be translated *the very end* or *last of days*. Here, Peter uses a form of the word *eschatos*, a term that depicts *what is final*, and it is where we derive the word "eschatology" — which is the theological study of end times or the ultimate end of a thing.

What's interesting is the word *eschatos* was used by ancient Greeks to describe the point that was furthest away. In the ancient world, people used the word *eschatos* as a seafaring word to describe the last port of call for a ship. Although a ship in transit stops at many ports en route to its final destination, the word *eschatos* was used to depict the very last port, and this last stopping-off point signified it was the end of the road and the journey was finished.

Furthermore, ancient writers used *eschatos* to refer to the final boundary of a territory, or the farthest edge of a domain. Thus, Peter's use of the word *eschatos* indicates this is the end, and one can go no further. In this verse, *eschatos* points to *the very ultimate end of days* or to *the very last of a long last-days season* that could be called *the last of the last days*.

'Scoffers' Will Arise

Peter is expressly describing the very end of the Church Age — when time has sailed to its last port, no more time remains for the journey, and we can go no further. At that moment in time, Peter says *scoffers* will arise.

In Greek, the word "scoffers" is *empaigmone empaiktai*, which would be better translated as *scoffing scoffers*, and this repeated emphasis indicates these individuals will be professionals at scoffing. This word is derived from a term that depicts those who make fun of something through mockery. It was often used to indicate the act of playing a game with children or amusing a crowd by impersonating someone in a silly and exaggerated way.

This word was also used to depict a game of charades when one intends to comically portray or even make fun of someone else. Peter used this word to foretell a day at the very end of the age before Jesus returns when scoffers would rise up to mock people who still believe in Christ's return for the Church. If you're hearing people question the Rapture or mock those who believe it's a real event that will soon take place, you are seeing Peter's prophecy fulfilled before your very eyes.

Factoring in the original Greek meaning of all these key words, here is the *Renner Interpretive Version (RIV)* of Second Peter 3:3:

> **Knowing, always knowing, and never forgetting — first, foremost, and above all else — specifically in the last of days, when time has sailed to its last port and not much more time is left for the journey, you'll know it because of mocking scoffers — those who sneer and make fun of those who believe in Christ's coming, people who are really dominated and ruled by their own base instincts and who are following after them.**

Scoffers Will Question and Mock 'The Promise' of Christ's Coming

So what are these scoffers going to be saying? Peter tells us they will be saying, "…Where is the promise of his coming? for since the fathers fell asleep, all things continue as they were from the beginning of creation" (2 Peter 3:4). Again, there are several key words to understand in this verse.

First is the word "saying" — the Greek word *legontes*. It pictures *one who says, says, and says* or *one who talks continuously*. The use of *legontes* here means these scoffers will be saying and saying and saying and saying, "…Where is the promise of his coming?" (2 Peter 3:4).

The word "where" is the Greek word *pou*, and it means *where*, *exactly where*, or *in what place*. It is used to question whatever is being discussed. These scoffers are specifically questioning "the promise of his coming." In Greek, "the promise" is the phrase *he epangelia*. This is the definite article *he*, and the word *epangelia* is the word for *an announcement, declaration*, or *guaranteed promise*. Interestingly, it was also a legal term to describe *what has been legally promised and is expected to come to pass*.

In this verse, however, Peter uses the definite article *he* to state that *THE promise* of Christ's return is a very specific promise that God has announced, declared, guaranteed, and promised to come to pass. The guaranteed promise of Christ's return was an integral part of apostolic preaching and teaching. They preached and taught it because they believed in the rapture of the Church.

Peter said that at the very, very end of the age, scoffing scoffers will arise who will keep saying and alleging, "Exactly where is THE promise of Christ's coming that has been announced, declared, and guaranteed?"

This brings us to the word "coming," which is a form of the remarkable Greek word *parousia*. It is a technical expression for *the royal visit of a king or emperor who has come with all the power, might, and authority to deal with a situation and put everything in order*. Without question, our world is in an unbelievable mess, and no person from a government program is going to fix it. Only Jesus has all power, might, authority, and wisdom to deal with every situation and put things in order.

It is interesting to note that the Greek word *parousia* is used interchangeably throughout the New Testament to describe both the rapture of the Church and the Second Coming of Christ. The way to know how *parousia* is being used depends on the context of surrounding verses. Here in this passage, Peter used it to refer to the long-promised rapture of the Church, which scoffers are mocking and questioning.

Scoffers Will Claim That Everything Continues To Remain Unchanged Since Creation

Looking once more at Second Peter 3:4, Peter tells us scoffers will be repeatedly saying, "…Where is the promise of his coming? for since the fathers fell asleep, all things continue as they were from the beginning of creation."

What *fathers* is Peter talking about? Well, in Greek, "the fathers" is *hoi pateres*, and this could refer to *the earliest fathers of the Christian faith*, who firmly believed in and declared the promise of Christ's return for the Church at the end of the age. At the same time, it could also refer to earlier fathers of the faith — as early as Enoch — who, from the very beginning of time, saw the end of the age and prophesied the eventual return of Christ (*see* Jude 14,15).

Peter said these scoffers will claim that "…all things continue as they were from the beginning of creation" (2 Peter 3:4). The word "continue" here is a form of the Greek word *diameno*, which means *to perpetually and thoroughly remain completely the same and unchanged*. Moreover, the phrase "as they were" is a translation of the Greek word *houtos*, which means *in keeping with, in like manner, in the same manner,* or *exactly the same*. Thus, it is something consistent and unchanged. Furthermore, the word "beginning," which is a form of the Greek word *arche*, describes *the beginning of creation* or what is *the most ancient and archaic of known time*.

Taking into account the original Greek meaning of the key words in this verse, here is the *Renner Interpretive Version* (*RIV*) of Second Peter 3:4:

> **They go on and on, alleging and saying, "Exactly where is the guaranteed promise of his glorious coming?" Those mockers will allege, "For from the time that the fathers died, absolutely everything continues perpetually the same and is unchanged — exactly as they have always been and in keeping with how they have been from the very beginning of creation."**

Those who scoff at the idea of the Rapture basically say, "Come on guys! People have been talking about Jesus returning to rapture the Church since the dawn of creation. It's nothing but pure fantasy — a pipe dream. You can kiss that idea goodbye and get on with life."

God Doesn't View Time Like We Do

Just a few verses later, Peter goes on to say, "But, beloved, be not ignorant of this one thing, that one day is with the Lord as a thousand years, and a thousand years as one day" (2 Peter 3:8). The word "ignorant" is a form of the Greek word *lanthano*, which means *to forget, deliberately ignore,* or *purposefully disregard*. Hence, it is the idea of completely forgetting facts that were previously believed or known.

In the context of Second Peter 3:8, Peter is urging his readers — which includes us — NOT to be ignorant of the truth. Although others are deliberately ignoring, purposely disregarding, and completely forgetting facts they previously believed about the rapture and Christ's coming, Peter is urging us not to ignore and release these truths.

He then adds, "...One day is with the Lord as a thousand years, and a thousand years as one day" (2 Peter 3:8). This tells us that God doesn't view time as we do. From His perspective, one day and one millennium are much the same, and time goes by very quickly.

Factoring in the original Greek meaning of the words in this verse, here is the *Renner Interpretive Version* (*RIV*) of Second Peter 3:8:

But it is vital that you don't ever forget or allow yourself to lose sight of this one very important thing. Beloved — those whom I deeply love and cherish — it is imperative that you never forget or lose sight of the fact that one 24-hour day before the Lord is just like 1,000 years — and 1,000 years is precisely like a single 24-hour day.

Essentially, God wants us to realize that in the whole scheme of things, time is very short, and the Lord's coming is extremely close at hand.

The Lord Is Not Slow or Tardy Regarding His Promise To Return

Peter then immediately adds, "The Lord is not slack concerning his promise, as some men count slackness; but is longsuffering to us-ward, not willing that any should perish, but that all should come to repentance" (2 Peter 3:9).

The word "slack" here is a form of the Greek word *braduno*, which means *to be tardy, slow, delayed,* or *late in time.* Here, it specifically refers to *lateness in reference to an appointed time.* The word *braduno* — translated here as "slack" — was also used medically to describe a person who was mentally or physically handicapped, and therefore slow to speak or slow in terms of physical movement.

Ancient Greek speakers also used this term to picture a person who is hesitant to act due to either a lack of direction, commitment, or resources. By using this word *braduno*, the Holy Spirit is stating God is **not** delayed, slow, or tardy regarding the promise that Jesus will return, or furthermore, regarding any promise of a coming future judgment.

Peter said the Lord is not slack concerning His promise "…as some men count slackness…" (2 Peter 3:9). In Greek, the word "count" is a form of *hegeomai*, which means *to conclude, consider, deem, esteem, figure,* or *suppose.* And the word "slackness" is again the Greek word *braduno*, meaning *to be tardy, slow, delayed, or late in time,* but specifically refers to *lateness in reference to an appointed time.*

Rather than be slow, delayed, or tardy in regard to Christ's return, Peter says the Lord is "longsuffering." This is translated from a form of the Greek word *makrothumeo*, a compound of *makros* and *thumos.* The word *makros* depicts *what is long or of long duration*, similar to a long span of time, while *thumos* describes *anger* and depicts *a strong and growing passion*. When these two words are compounded to form the word *makrothumeo*, it pictures *the patient restraint of anger and denotes longsuffering*. God is patiently restraining Himself from judgment, waiting for people to repent, not wanting a single person to perish for eternity. Although this doesn't mean everyone is going to repent, God wants to give everyone a chance to repent and receive the gift of salvation through Jesus Christ.

When we factor in the original Greek meaning of all these key words, the *Renner Interpretive Version* (*RIV*) of Second Peter 3:9 is as follows:

> **The Supreme Lord and Master — the One with authority in every known and unknown realm — emphatically and unequivocally does not delay, slow down, or show Himself to be tardy in any way concerning the promise [that He will return] — as some have concluded to be a delay, lateness, slowness, or tardiness (in keeping His promise) — but on the other hand, and all the way to the other end of the spectrum, God has chosen to hold out, to patiently wait, and to be longsuffering toward you. And He is not wishing for anyone to perish. On the contrary, God wishes that all would come to a place of repentance.**

Friend, the Rapture is real! Even though there are people that question, speculate, and mock those of us who still believe in Christ's imminent return to snatch the Church away, God is patiently waiting for that last person who's going to repent and then the Rapture will take place. You might be the person who leads that last person to Christ and then, *bam!* In the twinkling of an eye, we'll all be caught up into the presence of the Lord.

In our next lesson, we will take a detailed look at what the Bible has to say about the Rapture in Paul's first letter to the church of Thessalonica.

STUDY QUESTIONS

> **Study to shew thyself approved unto God, a workman that needeth not to be ashamed, rightly dividing the word of truth.**
> **— 2 Timothy 2:15**

1. Take a moment to read the context of Peter's warning in Second Peter 3:3-6. In addition to scoffers scoffing at the promise of Christ's

return, what two other monumental truths does Peter say people will deliberately forget (*see* vv. 5,6)? Are you seeing and hearing this happen in society? If so, where? What does this say to you about how close we are to Jesus coming back?

2. Essentially, the Bible makes it clear that God is patiently restraining Himself from judgment, waiting for people to repent of their sins (*see* 2 Peter 3:9). According to Ezekiel 33:11, how does God really feel about wicked people who die without repenting? What does First Timothy 2:1-4 say He would rather see happen, and what does He want you to do to help bring this about?

PRACTICAL APPLICATION

> **But be ye doers of the word, and not hearers only, deceiving your own selves.**
> —James 1:22

1. Peter prophesied that a major sign of the last days would be that scoffers would arise, questioning and making fun of those who believe in the promise of Jesus' soon return. Where are you seeing and hearing such mockery? Would you say this is decreasing or increasing in your lifetime?

2. How does the realization that we are living in the very ultimate end of the age or the last of the last days affect the way you see and live your life? If you knew that Jesus was returning to rapture the Church in the next 30 days, what would you do differently? What would you *stop* doing, and what would you *start* doing?

LESSON 3

TOPIC

The Rapture in First Thessalonians

SCRIPTURES

1. **1 Thessalonians 4:15-17** — For this we say unto you by the word of the Lord, that we which are alive and remain unto the coming of the

Lord shall not prevent them which are asleep. For the Lord himself shall descend from heaven with a shout, with the voice of the archangel, and with the trump of God: and the dead in Christ shall rise first: Then we which are alive and remain shall be caught up together with them in the clouds, to meet the Lord in the air: and so shall we ever be with the Lord.

2. **Luke 18:8** — …When the Son of man cometh, shall he find faith on the earth?

GREEK WORDS

1. "are alive" — **οἱ ζῶντες** *(hoi zontes)*: the living ones, the vibrant ones; not lifeless and dead

2. "remain" — **οἱ περιλειπόμενοι** *(hoi perileipomenoi)*: remaining ones; surviving ones; those who are left, indicating possibly not many; coincides with Second Thessalonians 2:2

3. "find" — **εὑρίσκω** *(heurisko)*: to find or discover; a discovery made as a result of careful observance; pictures a moment when one makes a conclusive discovery; usually points to a discovery made due to an intense investigation, scientific study, or scholarly research

4. "faith" — **τὴν πίστιν** *(ten pistin)*: with a definite article, the faith

5. "unto" — **εἰς** *(eis)*: unto; right unto

6. "coming" — **παρουσία** *(parousia)*: a technical expression for the royal visit of a king, or emperor; the arrival of one who alone can deal with a situation; used here to denote the coming of Christ for the Church

7. "not prevent" — **οὐ μὴ φθάσωμεν** *(ou me phthasomen)*: no, they shall not precede; from **φθάνω** *(phthano)*, to come before, to precede

8. "them which are asleep" — **τοὺς κοιμηθέντας** *(tous koimethentas)*: from **κοιμάω** *(koimao)*; to sleep; to sleep deeply; the sleep of death; where we get the words coma and catacomb

9. "descend" — **καταβαίνω** *(katabaino)*: compound of **κατά** *(kata)* and **βαίνω** *(baino)*; the word **κατά** *(kata)* means down and **βαίνω** *(baino)* means to step; to come down; to move downward from a higher place to a lower place; to descend; pictures downward movement with a dominating force

10. "from heaven" — **ἀπ᾽ οὐρανοῦ** *(ap' ouranou)*: directly from the heavens

11. "shout" — **κέλευσμα** (*keleusma*): a direct order or command; used to arouse horses, charioteers, hounds, hunters, rowers, masters of ships; a signal given like a trumpet call to muster troops to action

12. "voice" — **φωνή** (*phone*): voice; sound; noise; to whirl; depicts the sound of wind, wings, or water; may depict the sound of a massive multitude; an overwhelming sound

13. "archangel" — **ἀρχάγγελος** (*archangelos*): an archangel; from **ἄρχω** (*archo*) and **ἄγγελος** (*angelos*); the word **ἄρχω** (*archo*) means chief, foremost, leader, supreme, and indicates antiquity; the word **ἄγγελος** (*angelos*) in this case is a heavenly angel; compounded, it depicts one of the angels who is chief, foremost, leader, or supreme, and who has held this position since ancient times; probably Michael

14. "trump of God" — **σάλπιγγι Θεοῦ** (*salpingi Theou*): the word **σάλπιγξ** (*salpigx*) depicts a war trumpet that calls to war; a war trumpet that announces battle, ultimate victory, and the vanquishing of enemies at the very outset of a military campaign; used in the Old Testament for when God summons His people to war

15. "the dead in Christ" — **οἱ νεκροὶ ἐν Χριστῷ** (*hoi nekroi en Christo*): from **νεκρός** (*nekros/ne-kros*), a lifeless corpse

16. "shall rise" — **ἀναστήσονται** (*anastesontai*): from **ἀνίστημι** (*anistemi*), to stand again, to rise; to be resurrected; used to depict a rising of kings and rulers

17. "first" — **πρῶτον** (*proton*): first in order; in first place; to begin with

18. "then" — **ἔπειτα** (*epeita*): upon that moment; exactly at that moment; exactly then

19. "we which are alive" — **οἱ ζῶντες** (*hoi zontes*): the living ones; to be alive, not lifeless and dead

20. "remain" — **οἱ περιλειπόμενοι** (*hoi perileipomenoi*): remaining ones; surviving ones; those who are left, indicating possibly not many

21. "caught up together" — **ἁρπάζω** (*harpadzo*): catch, seize, or take away; to snatch suddenly; to snatch just in time

22. "clouds" — **νεφέλαις** (*nephelais*): plural, clouds

23. "meet" — **ἀπάντησις** (*apantesis*): to the meeting; to the reception; to the encounter; a technical word used for the reception of a newly arrived official or royalty

24. "air" — **ἀέρα** (*aera*): air; the lower regions of the heavens; the lower atmosphere

25. "ever be" — **πάντοτε** (*pantote*): at all times, all the time, always, continually, perpetually

SYNOPSIS

In our first lesson, we learned there are nine rapture-type events recorded in the Bible from Genesis to Revelation. Six have already taken place, and three are yet to come. The fact there are so many rapture examples found in Scripture refutes the misguided notion that the rapture of the Church is just a fantasy or wishful thinking.

In Lesson 2, we saw that Peter prophesied that at the very end of the age, when time has run out, scoffers will arise to question and ridicule those of us who believe Jesus is going to return and snatch His Bride away as the Bible teaches. The fact that there is a growing number of people — even in the Church — who mock the idea of the Rapture is in itself a sign we've sailed to the very end of the age.

In this lesson, we will closely examine First Thessalonians 4:15-17, which is the most detailed description of what will take place when Jesus comes to rapture His Church.

The emphasis of this lesson:

The teaching of the rapture of the Church is clearly stated in the Bible. First Thessalonians 4:15-17 says a day is coming when those who died in Christ will be raised to life and caught up into the air, immediately followed by the remnant of Christians who are still alive on the earth. Together we will be seized out of danger to meet Jesus in the air and be with Him forever.

The Concept of the Rapture
Is Clearly Conveyed in First Thessalonians 4:15-17

If you have ever wondered if the message of the Rapture was in the Bible, the passage you are about to read and hear explained in the original Greek may be the most valuable information on the subject you have ever received. Writing under the inspiration of the Holy Spirit, the apostle Paul shared with all believers what will take place when Jesus returns to gather His Church:

For this we say unto you by the word of the Lord, that we which are alive and remain unto the coming of the Lord shall not prevent them which are asleep. For the Lord himself shall descend from heaven with a shout, with the voice of the archangel, and with the trump of God: and the dead in Christ shall rise first: Then we which are alive and remain shall be caught up together with them in the clouds, to meet the Lord in the air: and so shall we ever be with the Lord.

— 1 Thessalonians 4:15-17

It is vital to note that when Paul wrote these words, they were not an idea he conjured up. On the contrary, he opens this passage by saying, "For this we say unto you *by the word of the Lord...*" (1 Thessalonians 4:15). This is the word of the Lord — not the word of Paul. To get a clear picture of what the Rapture is going to look like, let's dissect this passage, beginning with verse 15.

Those Who Are 'Alive and Remain' Will Be Raptured

For this we say unto you by the word of the Lord, that we which are alive and remain unto the coming of the Lord shall not prevent them which are asleep.

— 1 Thessalonians 4:15

Believers who *are alive and remain* will be the ones raptured by Christ. The words "are alive" are a translation of the Greek words *hoi zontes*, which describes *the living ones* or *the vibrant ones*. These are people that are not lifeless and dead.

The word "remain" is also significant. It is the Greek word *hoi perileipomenoi*, which is the very word used to describe *a remnant of a big piece of garment*. It can also be translated *the remaining ones, surviving ones,* or *those who are left.* This word possibly indicates that when Jesus returns, not many will be left on the earth who are spiritually alive and vibrant.

This idea is also communicated by Jesus in Luke 18:8 where He prophesied about His return saying, "...When the Son of man cometh, shall he find faith on the earth?" The word "find" is a form of the Greek word *heurisko*, which means *to find or discover*. This is a discovery made as a result of careful observance and pictures a moment when one makes a conclusive discovery.

The word *heurisko* usually points to a discovery made due to an intense investigation, scientific study, or scholarly research. Its use here indicates that when Jesus comes, the earth will be so void of faith Jesus will have to investigate and look intensely to find it. The word "faith" is *ten pistin* in Greek, and because it includes the definite article *ten*, it really means *the* faith or *the clear, sound teaching of Scripture*.

Even though faith will be hard to find when Jesus comes to rapture the Church, there will still be a thriving remnant of believers that has survived everything and has managed to remain vibrant and spiritually alive.

Jesus Has All Authority and Power To Set Everything in Order

The Bible says that those who will be raptured are "...we which are alive and remain unto the coming of the Lord..." (1 Thessalonians 4:15). The word "unto" is the little Greek word *eis*, which means *unto* or *right up until*. And the word "coming" is again a form of the Greek word *parousia*, which is a technical expression for the royal visit of a king or emperor. It is the arrival of one who alone can deal with a situation.

This word *parousia* can be used to describe the rapture of the Church or the Second Coming of Christ. The way to determine how it is used depends on the context of the surrounding verses. In First Thessalonians 4:15, it is used to denote the coming of Christ for the Church in the Rapture. When the Lord comes to gather believers, He will come with all authority and power and begin to deal with each situation and set everything in order on the earth.

To be clear, the remnant of believers who are alive right up until Christ's coming "...shall not prevent them which are asleep" (1 Thessalonians 4:15). In Greek, the words "not prevent" literally mean, "No, they shall not precede." Moreover, the phrase "them which are asleep" in Greek is *tous koimethentas*, which is from *koimao*, meaning *to sleep* or *to sleep deeply*, and it refers to *the sleep of death*. It is where we get the words *coma* and *catacomb*.

When we factor in the original Greek meaning of these key words, the *Renner Interpretive Version (RIV)* of First Thessalonians 4:15 says:

For we declare this to you by the word of the Lord: Those who are physically alive and who have survived everything — I'm talking about the remaining remnant that will still be left on the earth at the time of the coming of the Lord — that living and surviving remnant will not precede those who have already died.

Jesus Will Descend from Heaven Accompanied By Three Distinct Sounds

For the Lord himself shall descend from heaven with a shout, with the voice of the archangel, and with the trump of God....
— 1 Thessalonians 4:16

Notice the Bible says, "For the Lord himself shall descend from heaven..." (1 Thessalonians 4:16). The word "descend" here is a form of the Greek word *katabaino*, a compound of the words *kata* and *baino*. The word *kata* means *down* and carries the idea of a dominating force; and the word *baino* means *to step*. When the two words are compounded to form *katabaino*, it means *to step down, to come down, to move downward from a higher place to a lower place*, or *to descend*. This word pictures downward movement with a dominating force.

Here we see that Jesus Himself will step down and move downward from a higher place to the lower place of earth. Specifically, the Bible says He will descend "from heaven," which means *directly from the heavens*. When Jesus descends from the heavens, He will be accompanied by three things:

1: A shout — The word "shout" is from a form of the Greek word *keleusma*, and it describes *a direct order or command*. It is used to arouse horses, charioteers, hounds, hunters, rowers, and masters of ships. Moreover, this "shout" is a signal given like a trumpet call to muster troops to action. When this shout takes place at the time of the Rapture, Jesus — the Commander-in-Chief of all of Heaven's armies — will muster the heavenly troops to action.

2: The voice of the archangel — The Greek word for "voice" here is *phone*, which indicates *a voice, sound*, or *noise*. This word can also mean *to whirl* and depicts the sound of wind, wings, or water. It may also depict the sound of a massive multitude. In any case, it is an overwhelming, loud sound of the archangel.

In Greek, the word "archangel" is *archangelos*, a compound of the words *archo* and *angelos*. The word *archo* means *chief, foremost, leader*, or *supreme*, and indicates *antiquity*. The word *angelos* in this case is *a heavenly angel*. When these two words are compounded to form *archangelos*, it depicts one of the angels who is chief, foremost, leader, or supreme, and who has held this position since ancient times. Most likely, it is the archangel, Michael.

3: The trump of God — The phrase "trump of God" is a translation from the Greek words *salpingi Theou*. The word *salpingi* is from the word *salpigx*, which depicts *a war trumpet that calls to war*. This war trumpet was used to *announce battle, ultimate victory, and the vanquishing of enemies at the very outset of a military campaign*. This term was used in the Old Testament for when God summons His people to war.

The sounding of this war trumpet at the time of the Rapture means when it is blasted, God is declaring the final battle has begun. Furthermore, when this trumpet is blasted, it declares right from the very beginning that the war is finished, and God is about to really deal with his enemies.

The 'Dead in Christ Shall Rise First'

...And the dead in Christ shall rise first.
— 1 Thessalonians 4:16

The apostle Paul wraps up First Thessalonians 4:16 by telling us "...the dead in Christ shall rise first." The phrase "the dead in Christ" — *hoi nekroi en Christo* — in Greek — is from the word *nekros*, which describes *a lifeless corpse*. Here it is plural and signifies *the lifeless ones*.

When the Bible says, "shall rise," it uses the Greek word *anastesontai*, from *anistemi*, which means *to stand again, to rise*, or *to be resurrected*. What is interesting about this word *anastesontai* is that it was used to depict a rising of kings and rulers. According to Scripture, we are seen by God as kings and priests in His service, and in Christ's millennial reign, we will rule with Him.

Nevertheless, before the living remnant of believers is raptured, the dead in Christ will rise *first*. This word "first" is the Greek word *proton*, and it means *first in order, in first place*, or *to begin with*.

Considering the original Greek meaning of all the key words in this verse, here is the *Renner Interpretive Version (RIV)* of First Thessalonians 4:16:

For the Lord Himself will descend from Heaven to take charge with a mighty military command that will arouse the saints and galvanize God's troops to action. And along with that command, precisely at that time, will also be heard the immense voice of an archangel, and the blast of God's war trumpet to signal that the final battle, ultimate victory, and vanquishing of all God's enemies is about to occur. That war-trumpet blast will be the indication that God's enemies have lost their long-standing battle with Him and that He reigns victorious and supreme over everyone, over every situation, and over every realm — total victory! And exactly when that war trumpet sound goes forth, the dead in Christ will immediately stand upright on their feet as they are resurrected to a brand-new, resurrected, royal status. This resurrection will take place as a first priority before the next sequence of events takes place.

The Phrase 'Caught Up Together' Is *Harpadzo* in Greek and *Raptura* in Latin

Then we which are alive and remain shall be caught up together with them in the clouds, to meet the Lord in the air: and so shall we ever be with the Lord.
— 1 Thessalonians 4:17

This verse begins with the word "then" — the Greek word *epeita* — which means *upon that moment, exactly at that moment*, or *exactly then*. As soon as the dead in Christ are resurrected back on their feet, in that exact synchronized moment, "…We which are alive and remain shall be caught up together with them…" (1 Thessalonians 4:17).

The phrase "we which are alive" is the exact same Greek wording we saw in verse 15. It is the Greek words *hoi zontes*, which describes *the living ones*. It means *to be alive, not lifeless and dead*, and it signifies those who are still spiritually vibrant when Christ comes.

The Bible describes these living ones as those who *remain*, and the word "remain" is the same Greek word we saw in verse 15 — *hoi perileipomenoi*. It can be translated *remaining ones, surviving ones*, or *those who are left*, indicating possibly not many in number.

Faithful Christ followers who are alive at the time of His coming and have survived everything that has transpired shall be "caught up together." This phrase is a translation from a form of the marvelous Greek word *harpadzo*, which in the Latin Vulgate is translated *raptura* and is where we get the English word *rapture*.

Thus, the word rapture IS in the Bible.

The word *harpadzo* (*raptura* in Latin) means *to catch, seize*, or *take away*. It can also be translated *to snatch suddenly* or *to snatch just in time*, which implies that the rapture of the Church may take place in a very dark moment. Indeed, it is a rescue operation carried out by Jesus Himself, and He will snatch those of us who remain and are believers out of harm's way just in the nick of time.

We Will 'Meet' Jesus in the Air and Remain With Him Forever!

Where will we be "caught up together" (raptured) with the resurrected ones? The Bible says, "in the clouds," and the word "clouds" is the Greek word *nephelais*, which is the plural for *clouds*. It is there, in the air, that we will "meet the Lord."

The word "meet" here is quite remarkable! It is from a form of the Greek word *apantesis*, which means *to the meeting, to the reception*, or *to the encounter*. It is a technical word used for the reception of a newly arrived official or royalty.

Even the word "air" is important. It is the Greek word *aera* and describes *the air in the lower regions of the heavens* or *the lower atmosphere*. Once we are with the Lord, the Bible says, "…So shall we ever be with the Lord" (1 Thessalonians 4:17). The words "ever be" are a translation of the Greek word *pantote*, which means *at all times, all the time, always, continually*, or *perpetually*.

When we factor in the original Greek meaning of these key words, the *Renner Interpretive Version* (*RIV*) of First Thessalonians 4:17 is as follows:

> **Then at that exact synchronized moment, those who are still physically alive and who have survived everything — I'm talking about the remnant that will still be around and left remaining at this time — they will suddenly and supernaturally**

be snatched away out of imminent danger just in the nick
of time as the Lord instigates a divine rescue operation to
transport them into the clouds to join those who have been
resurrected. There in the air's lower atmosphere where the Lord
has descended to meet them, those who were raised from the
dead and the remnant who was supernaturally snatched out
of danger will encounter the Lord. And at that encounter, the
Lord will roll out the red carpet to give the new arrivals a royal
reception to match the VIP status He knows they deserve! Then
and after that, we will always — at all times and forevermore —
be with the Lord.

Without question, this teaching by Paul found in First Thessalonians 4:15-17
is a detailed description of the rapture of the Church. His use of the word
harpadzo — translated as "caught up together" in verse 17 of the *King James
Version* and "raptura" in the Latin Vulgate — is an undeniable reference to the
Rapture. It is a sudden, snatching away of the Church just in the nick of time.

In our next lesson, we will examine what Paul penned about the Rapture
in his first letter to the believers in Corinth. We will learn how it was a
"mystery" hidden from previous Old Testament generations and has been
revealed in the New Testament times for our benefit.

STUDY QUESTIONS

> Study to shew thyself approved unto God, a workman that
> needeth not to be ashamed, rightly dividing the word of truth.
> — 2 Timothy 2:15

1. In addition to First Thessalonians 4:15-17, what other verses from the
    Bible do you know that talk about the rapture of the Church?

2. Were you aware that when Jesus returns to rapture the Church, there
    will be **three distinct sounds** that accompany His arrival? In your
    own words, describe each of these sounds (*see* 1 Thessalonians 4:16).
    How do these details give you a more vivid picture of the Rapture?

3. Now that you know the phrase "caught up together" in First Thessa-
    lonians 4:17 is the Greek word *harpadzo* and the Latin word *raptura*,
    how does it help you better understand that the concept of the Rap-
    ture is indeed in the Bible?

PRACTICAL APPLICATION

But be ye doers of the word, and not hearers only,
deceiving your own selves.
— James 1:22

1. Overall, what new insights about the Rapture are you receiving from this lesson — especially from the *Renner Interpretive Version* (*RIV*) of First Thessalonians 4:15-17 and the definition of the Greek word *harpadzo*? Take some time to reread this valuable information.

2. When Jesus returns, the believers who are *vibrant* and *spiritually alive* will be raptured into Heaven. Would you describe yourself in this way — as a believer who's vibrant and spiritually alive? If so, what evidence in your life confirms it? If not, how would you describe your spiritual condition? Pray and ask God to show you the practical steps you can take to improve it.

LESSON 4

TOPIC

The Rapture in First Corinthians

SCRIPTURES

1. **1 Corinthians 15:51,52** — Behold, I shew you a mystery; we shall not all sleep, but we shall all be changed, in a moment, in the twinkling of an eye, at the last trump: for the trumpet shall sound, and the dead shall be raised incorruptible, and we shall be changed.

GREEK WORDS

1. "behold" — ἰδού (*idou*): bewilderment, shock, amazement, and wonder

2. "I shew" — λέγω (*lego*): I say, not show; mysteries are revealed by speech

3. "mystery" — μυστήριον (*musterion*): a mystery, secret; a secret once hidden, but now revealed

4. "sleep" — κοιμηθησόμεθα (*koimethseometha*): from κοιμάω (*koimao*); to sleep; to sleep deeply; the sleep of death; death; where we get the words coma and catacomb

5. "shall…be changed" — ἀλλαγησόμεθα (*allagesometha*): to change; to exchange one thing for another; to transform

6. "moment" — ἄτομος (*atomos*): an indivisible moment; split second; an instant; where we get the word atom; something tiny or microscopic

7. "twinkling" — ῥιπή (*rhipe*): twinkling; twitch; so fast it is almost undetectable

8. "trump" — σάλπιγξ (*salpigx*): depicts a war trumpet; a war trumpet that boldly announces victory and the vanquishing of His enemies at the outset of a military campaign; prophetically depicts that moment when a trumpet was blasted to instigate war and to declare intended triumph and victory even at the outset of a war campaign; used in the Old Testament for moments when God summoned His people to war

9. "dead" — νεκρός (*nekros*): a lifeless corpse; a cadaver with no life left in it; plural, corpses

10. "incorruptible" — ἄφθαρτος (*aphthartos*): something that is incapable of decay; that which is incapable of suffering the effects of wear, tear, and age; timeless, immortal, and indestructible

11. "shall be changed" — ἀλλαγησόμεθα (*allagesometha*): to change; to exchange one thing for another; to transform

SYNOPSIS

Just hours before going to the Cross to pay the penalty of death for our sins, Jesus comforted His disciples by telling them, "Let not your heart be troubled: ye believe in God, believe also in me. In my Father's house are many mansions: if it were not so, I would have told you. I go to prepare a place for you. And if I go and prepare a place for you, *I will come again, and receive you unto myself*, that where I am, there ye may be also" (John 14:1-3).

Friend, Jesus' promise to "come again" and "receive us unto Himself" is a reference to the *Rapture*. It is Christ's promise from His own lips that He will indeed return and rapture us, His Church. This is the next event to take place in the sequence of end-time events. In our last lesson, we unpacked what Paul wrote about this event in First Thessalonians 4:15-17. In this lesson, we will carefully examine what he said about the Rapture in First Corinthians 15:51 and 52.

The emphasis of this lesson:

The rapture of the Church, which was once a mystery, is now revealed! There will be one final generation of Christians that will not see death. Instead, they will one day be suddenly caught up in the air, along with resurrected saints and Christ Himself. When the last trump sounds, their bodies will be instantly transformed into immortal, indestructible beings.

A Review of First Thessalonians 4:15-17

In Lesson 3, we meticulously unpacked what the apostle Paul wrote about the rapture of the Church in First Thessalonians 4:15-17. Let's briefly review what we've learned so far about Jesus' soon return by reading through the *Renner Interpretive Version* (*RIV*) of each verse, beginning with First Thessalonians 4:15:

> **For we declare this to you by the word of the Lord: Those who are physically alive and who have survived everything — I'm talking about the remaining remnant that will still be left on the earth at the time of the coming of the Lord — that living and surviving remnant will not precede those who have already died.**

In First Thessalonians 4:16, the apostle Paul goes on to say, "For the Lord himself shall descend from heaven with a shout, with the voice of the archangel, and with the trump of God: and the dead in Christ shall rise first." When we insert the original Greek meanings of the words in this passage, the *Renner Interpretive Version* (*RIV*) of First Thessalonians 4:16 says:

> **For the Lord Himself will descend from Heaven to take charge with a mighty military command that will arouse the saints and galvanize God's troops to action. And along with that command, precisely at that time, will also be heard the immense voice of an archangel, and the blast of God's war trumpet to signal that the final battle, ultimate victory, and vanquishing of all God's enemies is about to occur. That war-trumpet blast will be the indication that God's enemies have lost their long-standing battle with Him and that He reigns victorious and supreme over everyone, over every situation, and over every realm — total victory! And exactly when that war-trumpet sound goes**

forth, the dead in Christ will immediately stand upright on their feet as they are resurrected to a brand new, resurrected, royal status. This resurrection will take place as a first priority before the next sequence of events takes place.

In First Thessalonians 4:17, Paul adds, "Then we which are alive and remain shall be caught up together with them in the clouds, to meet the Lord in the air: and so shall we ever be with the Lord." In this verse, the phrase "caught up together" is a translation from a form of the Greek word *harpadzo*, which means *to seize or to snatch out of danger just in the nick of time*. The use of this word indicates that those of us who are believers and are alive on the earth at the end of the age will be surrounded by extreme difficulty just before Christ returns. In that moment, He will descend from Heaven with a commanding, dominating force and grab us out of the natural realm and pull us into the supernatural realm. And we will meet the Lord in the air.

Taking into account the original Greek meanings of the key words in this passage, here is the *Renner Interpretive Version* (*RIV*) of First Thessalonians 4:17:

> **Then at that exact synchronized moment, those who are still physically alive and who have survived everything — I'm talking about the remnant that will still be around and left remaining at this time — they will suddenly and supernaturally be snatched away out of imminent danger just in the nick of time as the Lord instigates a divine rescue operation to transport them into the clouds to join those who have been resurrected. There in the air's lower atmosphere where the Lord has descended to meet them, those who were raised from the dead and the remnant who was supernaturally snatched out of danger will encounter the Lord. And at that encounter, the Lord will roll out the red carpet to give the new arrivals a royal reception to match the VIP status He knows they deserve! Then and after that, we will always — at all times and forevermore — be with the Lord.**

Friend, what these passages say are worth shouting about! The rapture of the Church is the next event that will take place on God's prophetic calendar, and then the Church age will end, setting the stage for the Tribulation.

The Rapture Is a 'Mystery'

In addition to First Thessalonians 4:15-17, the apostle Paul also wrote about the Rapture in his first letter to the believers in Corinth. Under the inspiration of the Holy Spirit, Paul wrote:

> **Behold, I shew you a mystery; We shall not all sleep, but we shall all be changed.**
>
> **— 1 Corinthians 15:51**

The first word Paul included in this verse is "behold," which is the Greek word *idou*, and it describes *bewilderment, shock, amazement, and wonder.* What Paul was about to say was so magnificent that he injected his own feelings into the text. The word "behold"— the Greek word *idou* — is the equivalent of Paul saying, "Wow! Wow! Hold on and listen to what I'm about to tell you because it's going to blow you away!" Paul was about to describe the resurrection of the dead and the rapture of the Church — something Jesus Himself had revealed to him.

He then said, "…I shew you a mystery…" (1 Corinthians 15:51). The words "I shew" is the Greek word *lego*, which would better be translated "*I say*." This is important to note because mysteries are revealed by speech, not by showing something.

As Paul continued to speak in his letter, he was unveiling a "mystery" to all his readers which includes us. This word "mystery" is the Greek word *musterion*, and it describes *a mystery* or *a secret.* It is *a secret that was once hidden, but now is revealed.* What is this mystery that was hidden? It is the mystery of the rapture of the Church!

'We Shall Not All Sleep, But We Shall All Be Changed'

When Paul said, "We shall not all sleep," he used the Greek word *koimethe-sometha*, which is from *koimao*, meaning *to sleep* or *to sleep deeply.* It is the same word he used in First Thessalonians 4:15 to describe *the sleep of death.* The word *koimao* is where we get the words *coma* and *catacomb.* Hence, it is describing *those who have died* — and in this case the deceased were Christians.

Paul wrote this to let us know that not everyone is going to die. There will be one generation of loyal Christ followers in the last of the last days that will not see death. Instead, they are going to be alive right up until the coming of Christ, and when He comes, they "shall be changed." This phrase is a translation of the Greek word *allagesometha*, which means *to change, to exchange one thing for another*, or *to transform*.

The use of this word tells us that the remnant of believers who are alive when Jesus returns are going to be snatched up suddenly into the lower atmosphere and exchange their physical, earthly bodies for a new kind of heavenly body. This exchange will be a miraculous, supernatural transformation.

When we insert the original Greek meanings of these key words, the *Renner Interpretive Version* (*RIV*) of First Corinthians 15:51 says:

> **What I am about to say will totally flabbergast you. But listen carefully, for I am going to tell you something that was previously an unknown mystery but has been revealed to us. Here it is — all will not die, but all — the dead and even the living — will be altered, changed, miraculously modified, and transformed.**

Our Transformation Will Take Place in a Microscopic Moment at the Last 'Trump'

In First Corinthians 15:52, the apostle Paul continues to unveil the rapture mystery, telling us how and when we will all be changed:

> **In a moment, in the twinkling of an eye, at the last trump: for the trumpet shall sound, and the dead shall be raised incorruptible, and we shall be changed.**

Notice the word "moment." It is a form of the Greek word *atomos*, and it describes *an indivisible moment, a split second*, or *an instant*. It is where we get the word *atom*, which denotes *something tiny or microscopic*. In this case, it is a microscopic, indivisible moment of time.

Paul defines this tiny moment of time as the "twinkling of an eye." In Greek, the word "twinkling" is *rhipe*, which describes *a twinkling* or *twitch*. It is something that happens so fast it is almost undetectable. We might even call it an eye twitch. That is how fast the Rapture of the Church is going to take place. It will be so expedient that it is almost undetectable.

The Bible says this will occur *at the last trump*. Once more, we see a form of the Greek word *salpigx*, translated here as "trump," the very same word Paul used in First Thessalonians 4:16. It depicts *a war trumpet — a war trumpet that boldly announces victory and the vanquishing of God's enemies at the outset of a military campaign*. This word was used in the Old Testament for moments when God summoned His people to war. When the last trump sounds, it will be a prophetic declaration by God that the final battle against evil is about to take place, and all His enemies are about to go down. Furthermore, this war trumpet is also God's declaration of victory over all His enemies from the beginning.

'The Dead Shall Be Raised Incorruptible and We Shall Be Changed'

Looking again at First Corinthians 15:52, it says, "…The trumpet shall sound, and the dead shall be raised incorruptible, and we shall be changed." Here again we see a similar description of what Paul stated in First Thessalonians 4:16 and 17. The word "dead" is from a form of the Greek word *nekros*, which describes *a lifeless corpse* or *a cadaver with no life left in it*. In this case, it is plural, meaning "corpses." First Thessalonians 4:16 lets us know that this refers to "the dead in Christ."

Scripture says the believers who have already gone the way of the grave will be raised "incorruptible." This is from a form of the Greek word *aphthartos*, and it describes *something that is incapable of decay* or *that which is incapable of suffering the effects of wear, tear, and age*. Amazingly, the dead in Christ will not stay dead. They will be raised incorruptible.

The word "incorruptible" actually describes how our physical bodies "shall be changed." Once more the Greek word *allagesometha* — translated here "shall be changed" — means *to change* or *to exchange one thing for another* or *to transform*. We will *exchange* our temporary, mortal bodies for timeless, immortal, and indestructible ones. And all this will take place in a moment, in the twinkling of an eye at the time of the rapture.

Considering the original Greek meaning of the key words in this verse, here is the *Renner Interpretive Version (RIV)* of First Corinthians 15:52:

> **In a moment — a split-second, indivisible atom of time as fast as the twitch of an eye — at the very last trump, that war trumpet will loudly sound to signal that the final battle, ultimate**

victory, and vanquishing of all God's enemies is about to finally happen. That blast will be God's way of letting everyone know that His enemies have lost their footing and long-standing battle with Him and that He reigns victorious and supreme in total victory!

In that flash, the dead will stand upright on their feet and will be resurrected to a brand-new, resurrected, royal status. And at that exact moment, they will miraculously receive new bodies that are incapable of decay and that will never again show the effects of wear, tear, and age — timeless, immortal, indestructible bodies. We who are still alive when all this happens will be supernaturally transformed as our old bodies are exchanged for new ones that also are incapable of decay and that will never again show the effects of wear, tear, and age. Our bodies will literally be altered, changed, miraculously modified, and transformed into timeless, immortal, indestructible bodies.

Friend, when the dead in Christ are resurrected and the Church is raptured, you're going to get the facelift of your dreams! In a microscopic moment that lasts about as long as an eye twitch, your body is going to be miraculously modified! Never again will you see or feel the effects of wear, tear, and age because the transformation will be eternal. And the resurrected body you receive will be very similar to the one Jesus displayed when He was resurrected from the dead.

When we pull together Paul's teaching in First Thessalonians 4:15-17 and First Corinthians 15:51 and 52, it is undeniable that the rapture of the Church is Bible doctrine. Even though people today may question it and mock those of us who believe in it, it is a rock-solid teaching of Scripture describing the most extraordinary, earth-shocking event in history that is soon to take place.

In our final lesson, we will examine the rapture of the Church juxtaposed with the Second Coming of Christ and see from Scripture how these are two distinctly different events.

STUDY QUESTIONS

**Study to shew thyself approved unto God, a workman that
needeth not to be ashamed, rightly dividing the word of truth.**
— 2 Timothy 2:15

1. Paul classified the rapture of the Church as a "mystery." For reasons
   unknown, the Lord chose to keep this event under wraps until the
   Church Age. Why do you think He kept this extraordinary catching
   away of Christians hidden during Old Testament times?

2. What other major teachings of the Bible were also once classified as a
   "mystery"? Consider these passages:
   • Romans 11:24 and 25; Colossians 1:25-27
   • Ephesians 5:30-32
   • Ephesians 6:19; Colossians 4:3

3. Have you ever wondered what your new, incorruptible body will be
   like? Jesus gives us a glimpse in His post-resurrection appearances.
   Take a few moments to look up these passages and carefully observe
   what Jesus was able to do that you also will be able to do in your
   heavenly body.
   • Luke 24:13-51
   • John 20:19-30; 21:1-15
   • Acts 1:3-9

PRACTICAL APPLICATION

**But be ye doers of the word, and not hearers only,
deceiving your own selves.**
— James 1:22

1. What new details about the Rapture did you learn from First
   Corinthians 15:51 and 52? How is this passage different from
   First Thessalonians 4:15-17? What facts does it add?

2. Just imagine! With multiple signs in the world confirming we're
   living in the last of the last days, *you* may be a part of the generation
   of believers who does not see death but is raptured into Heaven with
   Jesus! What is your reaction when you ponder the possibility of being
   caught away with Christ in the clouds?

3. How does the thought of exchanging your physical earthly body for a new, heavenly body that will no longer feel the effects of wear, tear, and age encourage you?

TOPIC

Key Differences Between the Rapture of the Church and the Second Coming of Christ

SCRIPTURES

1. **1 Thessalonians 4:17** — Then we which are alive and remain shall be caught up together with them in the clouds, to meet the Lord in the air: and so shall we ever be with the Lord.

2. **Jude 14,15** — And Enoch also, the seventh from Adam, prophesied of these, saying, Behold, the Lord cometh with ten thousands of his saints; To execute judgment upon all, and to convince all that are ungodly among them of all their ungodly deeds which they have ungodly committed, and of all their hard speeches which ungodly sinners have spoken against him.

3. **Matthew 24:36-41** — But of that day and hour knoweth no man, no, not the angels of heaven, but my Father only. But as the days of Noe [Noah] were, so shall also the coming of the Son of man be. For as in the days that were before the flood they were eating and drinking, marrying and giving in marriage, until the day that Noe [Noah] entered into the ark, and knew not until the flood came, and took them all away; so shall also the coming of the Son of man be. Then shall two be in the field; the one shall be taken, and the other left. Two women shall be grinding at the mill; the one shall be taken, and the other left.

4. **Matthew 24:29,30** — Immediately after the tribulation of those days shall the sun be darkened, and the moon shall not give her light, and the stars shall fall from heaven, and the powers of the heavens shall be shaken: and then shall appear the sign of the Son of man in heaven:

and then shall all the tribes of the earth mourn, and they shall see the Son of man coming in the clouds of heaven with power and great glory.

5. **Revelation 1:7** (*NKJV*): Behold, He is coming with clouds, and every eye will see Him, even they who pierced Him. And all the tribes of the earth will mourn because of Him....

6. **Zechariah 14:4** (*NKJV*): And in that day His feet will stand on the Mount of Olives, Which faces Jerusalem on the east....

7. **Acts 1:9-11** — And when he had spoken these things, while they beheld, he was taken up; and a cloud received him out of their sight. And while they looked stedfastly toward heaven as he went up, behold, two men stood by them in white apparel; which also said, Ye men of Galilee, why stand ye gazing up into heaven? this same Jesus, which is taken up from you into heaven, shall so come in like manner as ye have seen him go into heaven.

8. **1 Thessalonians 5:9** — For God hath not appointed us to wrath, but to obtain salvation [deliverance] by our Lord Jesus Christ.

9. **1 Corinthians 15:51,52** — Behold, I shew you a mystery; we shall not all sleep, but we shall all be changed, in a moment, in the twinkling of an eye, at the last trump: for the trumpet shall sound, and the dead shall be raised incorruptible, and we shall be changed.

10. **Matthew 24:21** — For then shall be great tribulation, such as was not since the beginning of the world to this time, no, nor ever shall be.

SYNOPSIS

Have you read about or heard someone teach on the Second Coming of Christ and the rapture of the Church and gotten confused? You are not alone. There are some passages in the Bible that can be difficult to understand. The fact is these are two different events. In this lesson, we will carefully walk through Scripture and discover some of the key differences between the Rapture and Christ's Second Coming.

The emphasis of this lesson:

The rapture of the Church and the Second Coming of Christ are two separate events. At the time of the Rapture, Jesus will come for believers in the air just before the Tribulation begins, and at the Second Coming, He

will come with believers to the earth at the Tribulation's end. The Rapture initiates and the Second Coming consummates the Tribulation.

Five Biblical Differences Between the Rapture and the Second Coming of Christ

As we said in the introduction, the rapture of the Church and the Second Coming of Christ are two separate events. When the Rapture occurs, it will initiate a period the Bible calls the Tribulation, which will last seven years. At the end of the Tribulation period, Christ will return visibly with His saints, and that is called the Second Coming. To help you grasp the difference between these two unprecedented events, here are some key distinctions to understand:

ONE:
When the rapture of the Church occurs, Jesus will return FOR His saints. At the Second Coming, Jesus will return WITH His Saints.

First Thessalonians 4:17 describes the Rapture, and here, Paul wrote, "Then we which are alive and remain shall be caught up together with them in the clouds, to meet the Lord in the air: and so shall we ever be with the Lord." Inserting the original Greek meaning of the key words into this verse, here is the *Renner Interpretive Version (RIV)* of First Thessalonians 4:17:

> **Then at that exact synchronized moment, those who are still physically alive and who have survived everything — I'm talking about the remnant that will still be around and left remaining at this time — they will suddenly and supernaturally be snatched away out of imminent danger just in the nick of time as the Lord instigates a divine rescue operation to transport them into the clouds....**

That is what will take place at the rapture of the Church. Jesus will come *for* His people.

On the contrary, at the Second Coming of Christ, Jesus will return *with* His people, the saints. This will occur at the end of the seven-year Tribulation. We read about this in the book of Jude.

> And Enoch also, the seventh from Adam, prophesied of these, saying, Behold, the Lord cometh with ten thousands of his saints; To execute judgment upon all, and to convince all that are ungodly among them of all their ungodly deeds which they have ungodly committed, and of all their hard speeches which ungodly sinners have spoken against him.
>
> —Jude 14,15

These two verses are simply packed with meaning, and when we insert the original Greek into the text, the *Renner Interpretive Version* (*RIV*) of Jude 14 and 15 says:

> It is amazing that even Enoch, the seventh from Adam, prophesied, foretelling in advance, about these and other events that would occur in the future, saying, "Behold, the Lord, and when He comes, He will arrive in the midst of ten thousands — innumerable numbers — of His holy people, who will be with Him."

> When the Lord comes, He will carry out the irreversible charge of guilt that Heaven's court has issued inescapably against all so-charged. In the same way a lawyer brings forth indisputable and undeniable evidence in a court of law, Heaven's court will present irrefutable and uncontestable evidence to prove a charge of guilt against the godless and all the irreverent actions — beliefs, words, and deeds — that irreverent sinners have committed and have spoken so abrasively and insolently against the Lord.

Clearly, what Jude describes here is not the Rapture, because Jesus is coming *with* His people. This leads us to the second major difference.

Two:
When the rapture of the Church happens,
Jesus will return in the air.
At the Second Coming, Jesus will return to the earth.

At the time of the Rapture, Jesus will come *in the air* to retrieve the saints and take them to Heaven with Him. His feet will not touch the earth. We see this confirmed in First Thessalonians 4:17, which again says, "Then we which are alive and remain shall be caught up together with them in the clouds, to meet the Lord *in the air*: and so shall we ever be with the Lord."

Once more, when we insert the original Greek meaning of the words into this verse, the *Renner Interpretive Version* (*RIV*) of First Thessalonians 4:17 in its entirety says:

> **Then at that exact synchronized moment, those who are still physically alive and who have survived everything — I'm talking about the remnant that will still be around and left remaining at this time — they will suddenly and supernaturally be snatched away out of imminent danger just in the nick of time as the Lord instigates a divine rescue operation to transport them into the clouds to join those who have been resurrected. There *in the air's lower atmosphere* where the Lord has descended to meet them, those who were raised from the dead and the remnant who was supernaturally snatched out of danger will encounter the Lord. And at that encounter, the Lord will roll out the red carpet to give the new arrivals a royal reception to match the VIP status He knows they deserve! Then and after that, we will always — at all times and forevermore — be with the Lord.**

At the time of the Rapture, Jesus will meet us in the air and take us to Heaven for a seven-year span of time. There, our works will be carefully examined by Christ Himself, and we will be rewarded accordingly (*see* 1 Corinthians 3:13-15; 2 Corinthians 5:10). We will also take part in the marriage supper of the Lamb. When this celebration is completed, Jesus will return *to the earth* with the saints to set everything in order and establish His millennial reign. This is the Second Coming of Christ.

Again, the Rapture occurs in the air, and Jesus does not come to earth. At His Second Coming, He returns to the earth.

Three:
The rapture of the Church is a *private*, clandestine operation.
The Second Coming of Christ is *public* and visible worldwide.

Another major difference between the rapture of the Church and the Second Coming of Christ is that the Rapture will be a *private* event that is exclusively for believers, and the Second Coming will be a *public* event that all the world will witness. This differentiation can be seen throughout the Scriptures, including Jesus' familiar discourse with His disciples on the Mount of Olives where He said:

> But of that day and hour knoweth no man, no, not the angels of heaven, but my Father only. But as the days of Noe [Noah] were, so shall also the coming of the Son of man be. For as in the days that were before the flood they were eating and drinking, marrying and giving in marriage, until the day that Noe [Noah] entered into the ark, and knew not until the flood came, and took them all away; so shall also the coming of the Son of man be. Then shall two be in the field; the one shall be taken, and the other left. Two women shall be grinding at the mill; the one shall be taken, and the other left.
>
> — Matthew 24:36-41

Notice the words "taken" and "left" in verse 40 and then repeated in verse 41. They help us determine whether the event Jesus is describing to is the rapture or the Second Coming. The word "taken" in both verses is a form of the Greek word *paralambano*, which is a term of endearment that means *to dearly take to one's side*. Jesus said, one worker — the one devoted in faith to Him — will be taken to His side, and another one will be left. This word "left" is also significant as it carries the idea of *desperation*. For those that are left on the earth after the Rapture, it will be a very desperate moment. These words are clearly connected with the clandestine or secret gathering of the Church in the air.

The Second Coming of Christ will occur seven years after the Rapture, at the very end of the Tribulation, and it will be visible to the entire remaining population of the world. Jesus clearly states this in Matthew 24:29 and 30 where He declares:

> Immediately after the tribulation of those days shall the sun be darkened, and the moon shall not give her light, and the stars shall fall from heaven, and the powers of the heavens shall be shaken: and then shall appear the sign of the Son of man in heaven: and then shall all the tribes of the earth mourn, and they shall see the Son of man coming in the clouds of heaven with power and great glory.

Note that in this passage, Jesus specifically identifies the timeframe as "after the tribulation of those days." It is *after*, or at the end, of the Tribulation when He will appear in the heavens and *all* the tribes of the earth will see the Son of man coming and mourn. This is Christ's Second Coming, and there is nothing secret about it.

This same public, worldwide event is described by the apostle John in Revelation 1:7 (*NKJV*). Here John excitedly announces: "Behold, He is coming with clouds, and every eye will see Him, even they who pierced Him. And all the tribes of the earth will mourn because of Him...." Again, we see some of the same exact wording from John: "every eye will see Him" and "all the tribes of the earth will mourn."

To be clear, when Jesus comes clandestinely to rapture the Church, no one who is caught up in the air and sees Him will be mourning. On the contrary, they will be celebrating because they were rescued from the impending wrath that is coming on the earth.

FOUR:
At the time of the Rapture,
Jesus will not touch the earth; He will arrive *in the air*.
When the Second Coming occurs,
Jesus will put His feet on *the Mount of Olives*.

Now, at the Second Coming, Jesus will return with innumerable numbers of His saints to deal with evil and set everything in order. Unlike the Rapture when He returns and meets us, His Bride, in the air, at the Second Coming, the Lord will return to the earth. The prophet Zechariah confirms this, telling us

> **Behold, the day of the Lord is coming... And in that day His feet will stand on the Mount of Olives, which faces Jerusalem on the east...**
>
> **— Zechariah 14:1,4 (*NKJV*)**

This fact is echoed in the New Testament in the book of Acts where the physician and historian Luke writes:

> **And when he (Jesus) had spoken these things, while they beheld, he was taken up; and a cloud received him out of their sight.**
>
> **And while they looked stedfastly toward heaven as he went up, behold, two men stood by them in white apparel; which also said, Ye men of Galilee, why stand ye gazing up into heaven?**

this same Jesus, which is taken up from you into heaven, shall so come in like manner as ye have seen him go into heaven.
— Acts 1:9-11

The place from which Jesus ascended and was raptured back into Heaven was the Mount of Olives (*see* Acts 1:12). The angels in Acts 1:10 and 11 confirm the prophet Zechariah's prediction that when the Lord returns *to the earth*, He will set foot on the very same mountain — rescuing the people of Israel, annihilating the antichrist and the false prophet, and establishing His kingdom headquarters in the city of Jerusalem. All these events will occur at the Second Coming of Christ, not the Rapture.

FIVE:
When the rapture of the Church occurs, Jesus will *deliver* His Saints.
At the Second Coming, Christ will *position* His Saints to rule with Him.

Contrary to what you may have heard, the Lord has no intention of His Church experiencing the wrath He will bring to those on the earth who have rejected Him. This is made quite clear in **First Thessalonians 5:9**:

For God hath not appointed us to wrath, but to obtain salvation [deliverance] by our Lord Jesus Christ.

The word "wrath" here is from a form of the Greek word *orge*, and it describes *anger, wrath, indignation*, and *punishment* beyond human comprehension. It is used 31 times in the *King James Version*. The fact that we are saved from the "wrath" of God (*orge*) through Jesus is reiterated by the apostle Paul elsewhere in Scripture, including these two passages:

For they themselves report about us as to the kind of reception we had with you, and how you turned to God from idols to serve a living and true God, and to wait for His Son from heaven, whom He raised from the dead, that is, *Jesus who rescues us from the wrath to come.*
— 1 Thessalonians 1:9,10 (*NASB*)

But God demonstrates His own love toward us, in that while we were still sinners, Christ died for us. Much more then,

having now been justified by His blood, *we shall be saved from the wrath of God through Him.*

— Romans 5:8,9 (NASB)

Although some have said, "Christians have always gone through hard times," the extreme difficulties that will take place during the Tribulation will not be like any other time in world history. Those are Jesus' words — not the words of any man (*see* Matthew 24:21). Again, "God hath not appointed us to wrath, but to obtain *salvation* by our Lord Jesus Christ…" (1 Thessalonians 5:9), and the word "salvation" here in the original Greek text means *deliverance.*

Remember, at the time of the Rapture, the Bible says we will be "caught up together" with Jesus in the air (*see* 1 Thessalonians 4:17). And that phrase means *to be seized or snatched out of danger just in the nick of time.* Just before the wrath of God begins to be poured out on the earth, Christ will snatch us up and receive us unto Himself so that where He is we will be also (*see* John 14:3).

Those Who Are Raptured Will Not Taste Death

In addition to being delivered from God's wrath, those that are raptured will also be physically delivered from death. We saw this previously in First Corinthians 15:51 and 52, where the apostle Paul wrote:

> **Behold, I shew you a mystery; We shall not all sleep, but we shall all be changed. In a moment, in the twinkling of an eye, at the last trump: for the trumpet shall sound, and the dead shall be raised incorruptible, and we shall be changed.**

When we factor in the original Greek meaning of the key words in this verse, the *Renner Interpretive Version* (*RIV*) of First Corinthians 15:51 and 52 says:

> **What I am about to say will totally flabbergast you. But listen carefully, for I am going to tell you something that was previously an unknown mystery but now has been revealed to us. Here it is — all will not die, but all — the dead and even the living — will be altered, changed, miraculously modified, and transformed.**
>
> **In a moment — a split-second, indivisible atom of time as fast as the twitch of an eye — at the very last trump, that war trumpet will loudly sound to signal that the final battle, ultimate**

victory, and vanquishing of all God's enemies is about to finally happen. That blast will be God's way of letting everyone know that His enemies have lost their footing and long-standing battle with Him and that He reigns victorious and supreme in total victory! In that flash, the dead will stand upright on their feet and will be resurrected to a brand-new, resurrected, royal status. And at that exact moment, they will miraculously receive new bodies that are incapable of decay and that will never again show the effects of wear, tear, and age — timeless, immortal, indestructible bodies. We who are still alive when all this happens will be supernaturally transformed as our old bodies are exchanged for new ones that also are incapable of decay and that will never again show the effects of wear, tear, and age. Our bodies will literally be altered, changed, miraculously modified, and transformed into timeless, immortal, indestructible bodies.

At the time of the Rapture, the dead in Christ will be raised back to life and given incorruptible, indestructible bodies. Immediately after they are raised and transformed, believers who are alive on the earth and spiritually vibrant will be caught up in the air to meet the Lord, and we, too, will be changed and given glorified bodies. Like Enoch, we will not taste death. Just as God took him suddenly, He will reach down and take us suddenly, snatching us out of the dangerous wrath to come.

The Rapture Will Trigger a Period Called the 'Day of the Lord' — a Time of Judgment That Will Last for Seven Years

Immediately after the rapture of the Church, it will trigger a period called the Day of the Lord, a time of judgment that will last for seven years. This period is also known as Daniel's seventieth week (*see* Daniel 9:20-27) and the time of Jacob's trouble (*see* Jeremiah 30:7). The moment the Church is vacated from planet earth, the Day of the Lord will begin, and for seven years, God will deal with the nations and the ungodly people of the earth who rejected Him. The world will experience a time of great tribulation such as never before. This is described by Jesus in Matthew 24:21, where He said:

> For then shall be great tribulation, such as was not since the beginning of the world to this time, no, nor ever shall be.

Friend, the rapture of the Church can occur at any moment. It is the next prophetic event to occur in the sequence of events here at the end of the age. Although no one knows the hour or the day, Jesus said we would be able to know the season of His imminent return by all the signs that will be occurring (*see* Matthew 24:1-14, 32-34).

The Second Coming of Christ will occur at the end of the seven-year Tribulation. Thus, its arrival will not be sudden and surprising like the Rapture, but predictable. After we, the Church, have spent seven years in Heaven with Jesus, enjoying the marriage supper of the Lamb and being rewarded for what we did for Jesus during our lifetime, we will return with Him to the earth. This is the fulfillment of Jude 14 and 15; Zechariah 14:1-5; Revelation 1:7; and many other prophecies.

Again, at Christ's Second Coming, He will destroy the antichrist with the brightness of His coming (*see* 2 Thessalonians 2:8), throw him and the false prophet into the lake of fire, and destroy all the kings and armies of the earth that gathered to make war against Him (*see* Revelation 19:19-21). Satan will be bound for 1,000 years, and Christ will reign in Jerusalem in His millennial kingdom.

STUDY QUESTIONS

Study to shew thyself approved unto God, a workman that needeth not to be ashamed, rightly dividing the word of truth.
— 2 Timothy 2:15

1. After working through this lesson, what details and scriptures were most helpful and eye-opening regarding the differences between the Rapture and the Second Coming of Christ?

2. Paul, Peter, and even Jesus Himself all described the rapture of the Church in a very unique way. To what did they all compare it? (*See* 1 Thessalonians 5:2; 2 Peter 3:10; Matthew 24:42-44; Revelation 3:3; 16:15.) Why can these passages not apply to Christ's Second Coming?

3. Knowing Christ's return to rapture the Church can happen at any moment, we must always be ready. What do these verses say we must continue to do to be ready for Jesus to come get us?
   - Luke 21:36 and First Thessalonians 5:2-10
   - First John 3:2 and 3 and Second Corinthians 6:14-18; 7:1

- Jude 20 and 21
- James 1:21-25 and Revelation 3:8,10,11

PRACTICAL APPLICATION

> But be ye doers of the word, and not hearers only,
> deceiving your own selves.
> — James 1:22

1. Have you been confused or fearful about Christ's return? How has this series — especially this lesson — brought peace to your heart and mind? What truths from Scripture might you share with a friend who has also battled fear and confusion regarding this topic?

2. Now more than ever, it is crucial that you be prepared for Jesus' soon return to rapture His Church. What action steps do you sense the Holy Spirit asking you to take right now to make sure you're ready? (Consider Hebrews 12:1,2.) What can you do to actively help others be aware and prepare for the Lord's return? (Consider 1 Timothy 2:1-4; 1 Peter 3:15; Jude 22,23.)

A Prayer To Receive Salvation

If you've never received Jesus as your Savior and Lord, now is the time for you to experience the new life Jesus wants to give you! To receive God's gift of salvation that can be obtained through Jesus alone, pray this prayer from your heart:

Jesus, I repent of my sin and receive You as my Savior and Lord. Wash away my sin with Your precious blood and make me completely new. I thank You that my sin is removed, and Satan no longer has any right to lay claim on me. Through Your empowering grace, I faithfully promise that I will serve You as my Lord for the rest of my life.

If you just prayed this prayer of salvation, you are born again! You are a brand-new creation in Christ! Would you please let us know of your decision by going to **renner.org/salvation**? We would love to connect with you and pray for you as you begin your new life in Christ.

Scriptures for further study: John 3:16; John 14:6; Acts 4:12; Ephesians 1:7; Hebrews 10:19,20; 1 Peter 1:18,19; Romans 10:9,10; Colossians 1:13; 2 Corinthians 5:17; Romans 6:4; 1 Peter 1:3

Notes

Notes

CLAIM YOUR FREE RESOURCE!

As a way of introducing you further to the teaching ministry of Rick Renner, we would like to send you FREE of charge his teaching, "How To Receive a Miraculous Touch From God" on CD or as an MP3 download.

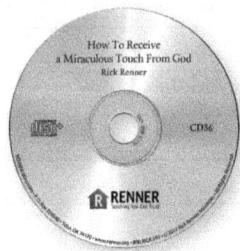

In His earthly ministry, Jesus commonly healed *all* who were sick of *all* their diseases. In this profound message, learn about the manifold dimensions of Christ's wisdom, goodness, power, and love toward all humanity who came to Him in faith with their needs.

☑ **YES, I want to receive Rick Renner's monthly teaching letter!**

Simply scan the QR code to claim this resource or go to: **renner.org/claim-your-free-offer**

Connect

WITH US!

🏠 renner.org

📘 facebook.com/rickrenner • facebook.com/rennerdenise

▶️ youtube.com/rennerministries • youtube.com/deniserenner

📷 instagram.com/rickrenner • instagram.com/rennerministries_
instagram.com/rennerdenise